THE MIND
OF THE REAL!
Poetic, Motivational, Life, Spiritual

JASON DESECKI

outskirts
press

The Mind of the Real!
Poetic, Motivational, Life, Spiritual
All Rights Reserved.
Copyright © 2017 Jason Desecki
v3.0

The opinions expressed in this manuscript are solely the opinions of the author and do not represent the opinions or thoughts of the publisher. The author has represented and warranted full ownership and/or legal right to publish all the materials in this book.

This book may not be reproduced, transmitted, or stored in whole or in part by any means, including graphic, electronic, or mechanical without the express written consent of the publisher except in the case of brief quotations embodied in critical articles and reviews.

Outskirts Press, Inc.
http://www.outskirtspress.com

ISBN: 978-1-4787-8216-2

Cover Photo © 2017 thinkstockphotos.com. All rights reserved - used with permission.

Outskirts Press and the "OP" logo are trademarks belonging to Outskirts Press, Inc.

PRINTED IN THE UNITED STATES OF AMERICA

Contents

Life 1
Sin of a Sinner 2
Hate 3
The End 4
The Drug 5
Losing My Mind! 6
Bottom of the Bottle 7
Temptation 8
The Best of Both Worlds 9
The Internal Scar 10
Unknown Loss! 11
Evil 12
Confidence 13
I Want More! 14
Change 15
Normal 16
Freedom 17
Betrayal 19
Separate Ways 20
The Ride of My Life 21
Analyze Me 22
Death Is Certain 23
Flow of Life 24
Tunnel 25
The Fork in My Life! 26
Fire of Love! 27
Two Steps Back! 28
Running 29
Money 30

My Life	31
Falling	32
Give Everything!	33
Step In to Me!	34
Depression	35
The Lion King	36
My Angel	37
Demented Minds	38
Breaking Down!	39
Higher	40
Giving Just to Get!	41
Live and Live On	44
I Never Ever Knew	45
Moving, Moving, Moving	47
The Mist of Doom	49
All Mine	57
7 x 12	61
Addiction	62
Learn!	63
Time	65
Crossover	66
The Mind of the Real!	67
Greed	69
Tomorrow	70
Drugs, No!	71
To Be Cleansed	72
So Far Down!	73
How About You?	74
Myself!	75

Outside These Walls	76
How Are You Today?	77
Dreamer	78
What If?	79
Winning Hands	80
Go Get It!	81
One Second!	82
Machine My Mind	83
Pieces and Problems	84
Give to Get	85
My Love	86
Take Care	88
No Maybes	89
The Good	91
Dreams	94
Five Months Ago	95
Never let you go	96
We don't know!	98
Rock Star	99
Status of life	100
The Kiss	103
On My Way	104
Saved	105
Enough Is Enough	106
True Love	107
Thirty-Eight Days	108
Enamored	109
The Plan	110
Myself	111

Paranoid	112
Me	113
Serenity	114
Wasted	115
Stand by Me	116
Take Me Away	117
Can't Stop Thinking!	119
Pain	121
In the Middle of Life	122
Words	123
Hard Times	124
Stuck Here	126
Positive Goals!	128
Drive Thru World	129
Breathe	130
Sunshine	131
Freedom	132
Decisions	133
Small Devices	135
Eighteen Days	136
Cash It In	137
My Civil War	138
Hold On	139
Destiny	141
Thirty-One Years To Be	142
Heartache	148
Boone County	149
Are They Coming?	150
These Days	151

At Ease	152
Faith	155
So Small Yet So Big	158
Tick Tock	163
My Queen	164
On My Way	165
Haters	166
Guidance	167
The Devil's Game	169
The Florida Keys	170
Both Ways!	171
This House Is a Circus	172
Vision	173
My Angel	174
Presence	177
Time Machine	178
Tomorrow	179
Time	180
Ego	181

Introduction

My life has been a learning experience. A journey to overcome and become! This book contains the past seven years of my life. Every poem and thought as written in this book is in order, from the first to the last! A seven-year bender with life! From heartache, loss, addiction, and being in and out of jail. Running from my problems and life! Lost in my own way! (Ego!) To self-motivation, and finding my higher power!

Becoming a Human being! Not a Human Doer!

Life has been a ride against time beyond the past seven years. Thirty-two!
Time is now present!
Life is Presence . . . Presents!

The Mind of the Real

This is my mind, my views, my thoughts, my troubles and defeats! With hard times come knowledge! This is my pain, my happiness, my inner feeling. In a motivating poetic standpoint you will feel my struggles with life, good, and evil. Take them in and learn how to overcome some of yours! From self-motivation, to heartache, to temptation, to being lost in one's own thoughts. These poems and thoughts I've written to overcome parts of my life that I've been through, and to prepare for tomorrow's best to worst deals. This is the mind!

The Mind of the Real!

See page 64. (For this page speaks many words!)

Life

Twenty-five. Where is it going? Where has it been? Life!
It's been a crazy ride through thick and thin! Life!
Will the crazy ride ever slow down in my life?
Do I really want it to? Life!

Sin is all around me but that is life!
I love to taste sin but not overindulge for it will ruin my life!

Who knows where it lies? The answers to life!
If I found them would I really want to know? Life!
Some believe it lies in the palm of your hand! Life!
There are times I feel like I sold it to the
man downstairs, my life!
Those are the rock bottom moments in my life!
What side of the TV is real? Life!
Will I find my channel to my life?
This is the life I live and the life I love!
But unknown when to leave this
LIFE!

Sin of a Sinner

Sin is there, but for me no fear,
For sin should have a fear for me!
I walk this world tall and strong,
But sin always gets in my way!
I take sin on the walk with me,
But sin will not let go!
I'm a sinner through and through,
The sin I will always hold!

Hate

Hate, it's what you did to me, Hate!
I can't set it free, Hate!

It tells me lies, Hate!
It makes me cry, Hate!

Its blood, sweat, and tears, Hate!
It's what gives me no fear, Hate!

It eats inside of me, Hate!
But at the same time it eats outside of you, Hate!

The more you feed it the more you want to do, Hate!

It's a powerful thing, it will drive you insane, Hate!

Can I ever let it go? Hate!

Not even with time will I know!

HATE!

The End

The near is here the end is near!
I am getting closer and closer it is near.

Don't be afraid don't show no fear,
For the near is here the end is near!

When you get there show pride,
Courage, and strength beyond belief for the end
could be under your feet!

When the end is there, you will never know,
But it's always near and will always show!

The Drug

It lives within, but not without.
I love this drug, without a doubt!

This is the drug of drugs that gets me higher!
This is the one that I desire!

To the highest peak or the valley low,
This drug is there and will never go!

This drug is pure this drug is real.
I love how this drug makes me feel!

I take this drug any way I can!
But keep it in me for who I am!

This is a drug that gets me higher with time.
This drug is real, this drug is fine!

Losing My Mind!

Look through the walls, look through your eyes!
Look closer now, can you find me?

Come on, look closer now!

Look through the walls, look through your eyes,
Can you find me?
Can you find me?

I am running from you, hurry, I'm ready to hide!
Look through the walls, look through your eyes; hurry,
you are losing me!

You are finally inside, but which way should you go?
Hurry, you are losing me!

There are so many doors to choose from!
Which one should you choose?

I am fading now! I am so far gone!

You have lost me now!

You have lost my mind!

Bottom of the Bottle

As you sit at the bottom of this bottle
wondering how you can get out!
Looking up through that small hole
as if you were looking in a mirror!

How did you get there?

Can the image in the mirror get you out?

Maybe that image is afraid to let you out!
As for the fear that he is just going to put you back in!

The image feels at ease and serenity as it stares at you at the
bottom of that almost empty bottle!

At this point the image will do anything to keep you there!

Wow, he feels so good and is becoming more and more gone!
He slowly forgets about you sitting at the
bottom of that empty bottle.

The image no longer has a hold of the bottle.
And the bottom of the bottle now has a hold on you!

Temptation

This world is a place that is more evil and dark
than it is pure and bright!

The temptation to do evil and dark things
haunts me everyday!

I love temptation for it is something I can't control!

To me, temptation is the devil and the devil loves to test me!

Temptation is hell and hell is on earth!

So lie, lie to myself, let it take control!

Lie!

That is a powerful thing!

Temptation is so strong it has made me a liar!

But if I'm a liar, why can't I lie to temptation?

Get into temptation's mind, change him!

Change him before he changes you!

But, be careful, you might like what you see in there.

For it is the mind of

Temptation!

The Best of Both Worlds

I live in one, but love another!
I cross over sometimes to the other!
These worlds are different, but both very much mine!
Which one do I love the most?
I will someday know!
I love to watch these worlds grow!
One I live in, the other I dream!
The one I dream is becoming more real to me!
This is like saying dreams come true,
But it's the world I live, I no longer pursue!
So what I have dreamed and fantasized for so long,
is what I wanted all along!
So this is what it's like when both worlds collide!
The best of both worlds!
I'm trapped inside!

The Internal Scar

To be cut leaves pain and with pain there's time.
With time there's healing, after healing there's a scar.
The scar is there to remind you of the healing,
the pain, and the cut!
So how do we forget?
The scar is at one with your thoughts now!
The scars you don't see are internal.
These are the ones that eat at you without seeing!
Internal scars can destroy a man.
You must stop the feeding before there's nothing
left for the scar to eat!
You must get inside to fight it, put it down
so it never gets back up.
This can be a very long process!
Some never succeed to beat their internal scars and with
time those scars you couldn't see are now
there for the world too!

Unknown Loss!

As it flies out the window you are looking
in the rearview mirror
wondering, where did it go?
And who will find it?

Should I stop now and turn around to pick it up?
I'm not sure what it was!

It's a terrible feeling to have an unknown loss!

When I figure out what it was, can I replace it?
Will I be better off with it gone?

Keep on trucking and have my brain meltdown
with an overload of questions?

Maybe turn around and just take a peek.
Just to clear the head! But this may be a waste of time!

Speed away, don't look back!
Don't be a coward of your unknown loss!

Who knows, maybe down that road
your unknown loss will be right in front of you
And not a loss at all!

Evil

It's feeding on me, it's feeding on you!
It wants inside, don't know what to do!

It's feeding on me, it's eating me alive!
What will happen when it gets inside?

Will it take over me?
Will it eat my soul?
When it is done will it ever go?

It's feeding on me!
It's feeding on me!
It's almost in!
It's so hungry!

It can't get enough of me!
It wants me whole!

It is evil!
It's now inside!
It is evil and will not hide!

Confidence

Don't stop till you get it!
Don't ever give up!
Be confident in what you want for you will get it!
Tell what you want that you are the one and you will be mine!
Don't stop till you get it!

Confidence!

If you don't have confidence you don't have yourself!
You will never succeed in gaining what is yours!
So get a grip on yourself and don't let go!
Tell confidence that you are mine!
Take confidence in and keep it there!
Now don't stop till you get it!
You will always get what you want
as long as you got
Confidence!

I Want More!

I want more!
More I say!
That's right, I want more!
You give me a taste, the taste likes me!
That's right, I want more!
Call me greedy, call me insane!
That taste is in my brain!
I want more!
More, I say!
A little became a lot, but more is not enough!
Damn!
I love this stuff!
I want more!
Will I ever be satisfied?
I want more!
More, I say!
I'm addicted to more!
More, get away!
The addiction is more and the taste won't fade!

I WANT MORE!

Change

Everybody wants a change.
Change you!
Maybe they need to change them!
Who's going to do that? You!
People only change if they want to!
You are who you are!
So change for what? Somebody else!
Never!
We change our hair, our clothes, even our minds!
But we should never change our souls!
Our souls are roads to change!
Change will come to you when you get to change!

Normal

Who is normal?
Is there such a thing?
What is normal?
Where is normal?
Normal is locked up!
I have yet to find it!
The evil of mankind, maybe that is normal?
The kindest and most pure of mankind?
Maybe that is normal?
Am I normal?
Would I want to be normal?
Normal is a mystery to me!
Normal is a lock and nobody has a key!

Freedom

To do as I please keeps my mind at ease!
It is freedom!
Don't ever let it pass me by, don't ever give it away!
Be careful now, it can be taken away so fast, just as fast as it was giving!
It is freedom!
Life isn't as free as it should be, but it could be worse!
To be free, that is me!
I treat it as a gift!
The gift of freedom is the best of all.
Treat freedom with respect and you will have it all!
Freedom!

It is just a pill, how much harm could it be?
So I took it and it set me free!
It took me inside with it and it opened me up!
It spun me all around, made me feel so alive!
It was the beginning to a new life!
This pill was designed for me and it had a plan.
It made it inside of me and showed me love, lust, and who I am!
This pill searched deep within me and pulled it out!
I hope there is still some left in me for when this pill I'm without!

Betrayal

I took you in, I showed you love!
I trusted you as if you were me!
I was your friend, the best I could be!
You lied and showed me no respect.
I look back on it all and reflect!
How can someone take from someone and hide it so long?
I knew it was gone all along!
It just took time to see what you did to me!
Our bodies and minds have a way to hide pain from oneself!
You did to me what I would do to no one else!
Betrayal!
This is something you could never forget; once betrayed you could never trust again!
Betrayal is now there, it is always in.
Learn from betrayal and it will never happen again!
Betrayal!

Separate Ways

I am night and you are day!
So I got to go away!
My love for you will always stay!
We got to go our separate ways!
Will we be OK?
No one knows!
The separate ways are where the stories are told!
Let's go those ways and find our stories!
Someday soon we will find the glory to a new life for night and day!
It can all be found on our separate ways!

The Ride of My Life

Let's take a ride, come with me!
Open the door and you will see!
Get inside, don't be afraid!
This ride happens everyday!
The roads I take are not the same!
You'll see, my love, you'll feel my pain.
You'll touch my heart, you'll think my brain!
We can go fast or we can go slow!
No one knows where this ride will go!
This ride is me.
This ride is my life.
Come on!
Come inside!
Take the ride.
The ride of my life!

Analyze Me

Follow me, yeah!
Into my mind let's take a look at what's going on inside!
Do you like what you see?
Is this the mind of insanity?
Can you figure it out?
Diagnose me!
Don't get lost because you won't get out!
You're the one who is supposed to figure it out!
You're the shrink, the one who is going to analyze me!
Tell me, Doc, do you like what you see?
Another world in there beyond belief!
Don't visit too long; you won't come out the same.
You're getting lost inside my brain!
This journey is full of surprises.
How does one deal with this while he analyzes
the mind of the real?
Tell me, Shrink, do you like what you see?
Do you like how you feel?
Do you need a shrink just to deal with what you saw?
Or maybe I am normal and you are way off!

Death Is Certain

I hurt inside and out!
These are pains I can live without!
Death is all around me!
Pain is telling me to slow down, but I choose to continue my ways! Why?
Maybe death is my answer!
Death, do you like me?
Death, do you want me all to yourself?
I enjoy life, but at the same time I'm destroying it, or getting closer to it!
Getting closer to what?
Life after death or life with death?
Death, should I fear you, or will you take better care of me than my own life?
Some people want to meet you sooner than others!
Others have no idea when or where they will meet you,
But they know they someday will!
Death is certain!
Life is not!
Death must be a wonderful thing,
Because everybody gets to experience it!
Is the experience wonderful for everybody?
Or is it a lot like life?
It is what you make of it!

Flow of Life

What are you going to do?
How are you going to do it?
Make up your mind!
Figure it out!
What are you going to do with your life?
Why should you have a plan?
Can't you just go with the flow?
The flow of life, which direction is that?
Do you really want that?
Why didn't you get a plan when you were born?
Some directions, if you will!
It seems as if some did and some didn't!
The ones who didn't must be in some kind of test!
The test of what?
The test of life?
The ones who did are weak and will never learn from life!
So go with the flow; the flow of life and the direction it will take you
are entirely up to you!
Learn from the mistakes, for they will only make you wise!
The flow of life will eventually come to an end!
At that point you will be the one with the directions!

Tunnel

Crawling through the tunnel it's dark and gray. No clue how long it is or how dark it will stay! Just hoping I'm almost through, a little light if you will, I can't wait to get out to once again, feel how great it is to be on my own two feet again and how free I will feel on the other side! So just when I thought I was almost through I got around that curve still nothing in front of me still too dark to see! Keep on crawling, don't give up! That light is there, I will soon see it! This tunnel is my life, I got to believe in it!

The Fork in My Life!

Our decisions we make are unknown endings! So you really don't know if you're making the right decision till you get to the end! Like the fork in the road! The unknown way to go! You choose right but the whole time you're wondering if you should have taken a left! There comes a time when your decisions can be life changing! This is the fork in my life. The fork in my life is not as easy as the fork in the road! With the fork in my life I make a decision and it's not guaranteed I can turn around! I might be stuck on that decision I choose till the end! But with the fork in my life I can not do what I did with the fork in the road and that is turn around or wonder if I'm going the right way. That would only stop me from getting to the end and seeing the outcome of my decision!

Fire of Love!

I look at her and I feel it. The warmth all over the inside of my body! It's so real, I know! With all the hurt and hate I once had it's overpowering these feelings! My heart was broken but it has now repaired itself. The feelings deep in every chamber allow it to beat for her again. It is pumping the love throughout my entire body! I feel alive! Like a flame to a high flammable liquid, it burns so hot and strong! My love for her has become an uncontrollable fire within my heart. I believe there is nothing that can stop this furious fire of love that my heart has created for her! It began as a spark and started to grow. It got hungrier and found its fuel to burn for her! That fuel was a combination of time, heartache, and confusion! These three things ignited that spark and made my heart realize that this fire burning, so hot and strong, is love for her that I will always have. So I will let it burn just like an uncontrolled fire! Let it take down anything that gets in its way and this flame that is burning called love will only grow stronger for her and will burn in me for eternity!

Two Steps Back!

As I entered! A glimpse of my new life! It hit me how empty and plain it was! This new spot called home was just the beginning! In time it will grow into a palace of dreams and happiness! It looks like a small step but in reality it's the biggest step of my life! Two steps back and a lifetime of steps forward! Patience will be the key to moving forward! With that the palace will become my castle and my dreams will become my reality!

Running

Running so far away from it all! Nowhere to hide, just running blind. Run to the end! The end of my life! Run through the days! Run with the nights! Is this the way I am running for? Run, run, and run till I can't run anymore! Going to run so far ahead of my life then stop to take a look at it all! Running out of time! Don't run too far ahead, it will be too hard to find! This path that you are running on holds the future and the past! Run ahead to see what's coming, run back to see what I have passed!

Money

It is so dirty! Dirtier than the hands it passes! It is very stressful! It could only buy you temporary happiness; it is our ruin! Money! People kill for the green! Money! We work so hard for it then we just give it away! Everybody loves to get paid! Money! We love what we hate because we are nothing without it! Life should be called Money!

My Life

It's what they want me to do, it's how they want me to live! It's my life! It's how they want me to act, it's how they want me to speak! It's my life! They keep on pushing me! They keep on taking from me! It's my life! It wants me to be free! Come and set it free! It's my life!

Falling

Fallen from the edge of the sky! Fallen from the edge of my life! Don't let go of the sky, hang onto your life! Once you have a grip on it, reach beyond and try to grab the moon and move the stars!

Give Everything!

Living is the hardest thing when you got to give everything to survive! In this life you choose but refuse to change!
>Give Everything!
>Give Everything!

To me, make it all mine! Open up the doors, open up my mind to my dreams! Let me have control! Please someone show it to me! I will take it all! Never let it go!
>Give Everything!
>Give Everything!

To me! Come on, make me shine in this world of mine!
>Give Everything!
>Give Everything!

Step In to Me!

Take a step, a step into me. Take a step and you will see! Take a step into my shoes. You got nothing to lose! Take a walk, a mile in my shoes, maybe a block will do! Take this walk that I take in pride! These shoes have nothing to hide! Take a walk, take a walk with sin! I'll do it again and again! Take a walk with me! Do you like how they fit? One size doesn't fit all, look out for the shit! These shoes are my life! They grew on me! So don't ever try to step into me!

Depression

There's a feeling inside of me! Deep down inside of me! This feeling will never go! It is ticking and ticking! Look out now, it's ready to explode! I'm going insane, it's tearing my brain, and I haven't even lost control! I can't make it out! Just scream and shout! Cry my life away! Somebody come now! And try to save me! From this depression that is taking over me! Yeah this depression! Why are you here? Cry my life away!

The Lion King

Everything is clear now! Life is getting brighter! I've gotten back up and brushed myself off! Always prepared to fall! So the pain isn't so bad! As I journey into my new life I read people like an eagle to a field mouse at 300 yards away! Analyzing them and selecting them as if they are my army and ready for war! But at the same time not trusting anybody or allowing them to get to close! This world is my jungle and I am king! One step ahead! Never to be fed upon or used by any man or woman! This world holds billions of people but I see it through only one set of eyes and those are mine, therefore the world is mine! The world is my jungle I must go through it prepared for the worst! This will only make me stronger and bad days better!

The lion king!

My Angel

When I look at you looking at me! You see the demons! You're going to set them free! Heaven and hell, fallen in love! You have fallen into my hell! Take me away! Put out this fire! You're my angel! The one I desire!

Demented Minds

Twisting, turning, demented minds!
Walking, running out of time!
In and out our minds we go!
This is my mind that I yet know!
Minds are time! Time is always on my mind!
Go slow or go fast, time is burning! The mind is at waste!
Take that time and find a place!
Twisting, turning, demented minds. They all are beautiful
and come in time!

Breaking Down!

Breaking down! Down! Down! I have fallen to the floor, I have shattered into dull pieces! Many small, hard-to-see, or find pieces!

Breaking down! Down! Down! Never to be put together, only rebuilt! Never to shatter! Never to break down! Down! Down!

Higher

Higher than I want to be. This was the life for me! Higher than I ever been, I did it again and again! I got to get away!

Higher isn't going to let me be the man I am and sobriety! Higher, don't ever let me back into your world of darkness and sin!

I got to get away!

Higher, you stole from me but I have taken from you! The highest moments that I have ever been! Has created the man I am!

Giving Just to Get!

Giving just to get! This world is full of shit! Gotta get out before it gets too deep! I got everything I need!

                Giving just to get!

                Giving just to get!

Got to go so far away! Looking for tomorrow, tomorrow a better day!

                Giving just to get!

                Giving just to get!

Nothing is for free! Unless you take it away from you or me! Stripping the souls from others, giving them away for the dollar!

                Giving just to get!

                Giving just to get!

I woke up this morning and I had no soul! Where did you, where did you go? Are you alive or am I dead?

Come back, come back to me!

Who said you can be set free! I believe you were taken from me! I didn't sell you and I didn't trade!

Come back, come back to me!

Life without you isn't the same!

It's time to write my mind out my cravings, my aching heart, my long-lost mind! To put it all on paper! My life! A piece of paper! What, my soul can be read? How? So there's a life after I'm dead? A Bible!

Live and Live On

    I never knew the beginning! I never knew the end! To this life I'm playing! Live and live on!
>Live and live on!
>Live and live on!
>Yeah!

Brighter days, darker nights! Is this future dark or bright?
>Live and live on!
>Live and live on!
>Yeah!

Running through the nights, looking for the days. Life is passing me by. Got a head full of grays!
>Live and live on!
>Live and live on!
>Yeah!

I Never Ever Knew

I never ever knew! Never ever saw! Never ever got too involved! With this life I love but refuse to change! Never knew right from wrong. Always thought it was the same!

I never ever knew!

I never ever saw!

I never ever got too involved!

Now I'm getting older and I don't fucking know where my life is going to go! I'm getting older and I don't want it to end! Got to figure it out and start over again!

I never ever knew!

I never ever saw!

I never ever got too involved!

I'm breaking down, I'm breaking down. I never knew! I never knew!

Life is love, and love's with you! Loving you is love for me!

I'm breaking down, I'm breaking down! To this life, I must set you free! I never knew loving you was killing me! We learn from our mistakes everyday! Some you can hide and some you can change!

Moving, Moving, Moving

Life is always moving! Even when it stops it is still moving!
Maybe not for you but for somebody else!
Moving, moving, and moving!
What direction is life moving? Some are moving backward just to dwell and live in the past! Some are moving forward just to run to the end!
Moving, moving, and moving!
Life is always moving and will always last!

You only get one life! No maybes. You got to keep moving and changing. Life could be so good and amazing! You got to take a chance now, Oh Baby!

Life could be too short, don't be afraid; living for tomorrow, remember yesterday!

The Mist of Doom

I'm walking through the mist; it's thick and gloomy! Doom, doom, doom! No more till the end of time—my time! My time is now the beginning and the end of doom! My story is yet to be told; the mist is thinning now, the world I will hold! Doom, doom, doom! No more till the end of time—my time! I'm walking the line crooked and uncut! The toughest and sharpest, and bluntest! Slicing through the mist, so thick and so heavy, so solid and strong! I'm walking the line, getting straighter every step, the mist brighter and the doom to be gone! The mist of doom is unknown, how long? Every step closer to the beginning and the end! Why did I walk through the mist when I could have ran!

One day in! One day out!

The beginning to a new life. The best without a doubt.
Day by day, night by night! One at a time! I'll get this right!

When I get through all of this madness!
When I get through all of this pain!
That will be my day!
When I will shine again! There is a light at the end of this madness. That light will help me through my sins!
I will shine again.

Where would you be now, baby? Where would you go?
Where did you run and hide; I want to know!
I've been searching my whole life, baby!
When will you show!
Time is just my beginning to my rose!

The decisions I made, are they right for me?
Hopefully I'll someday see!
Today they feel like rough times and misfortunes!
Not even a cookie can tell me my fortune.
The road less traveled is the one I took!

Loving you every day now, baby. Loving you driving me crazy!
Loving you is so easy!
Ever since the day I met you! I knew that I would get you!
I never knew how much it would be! This love, it's so free!
Please baby, don't you leave me! I'm begging you, come on baby!
My heart is aching oh so badly! Oh baby! I'm so sorry! But you are so sick of that story! Please, baby, don't you leave me!
Oh baby, please don't leave me!
This love, it's so free!
Never knew what it would be! Just knew it was for me! I want it now, I want it back, I want it now! Oh baby, I want it now!
Never wanted this to end! Let's start from the beginning!
Loving you every day now, baby!
Loving you driving me crazy!
Loving you is so easy!
This love is so free!

I got this feeling deep inside me!
I got this feeling, I can't hide it!
I got a feeling that you want it!

Oh come on, please take it! It gets me higher than I want! You would love it without a doubt! Oh come on, please take it!
I can't have it, I'm retired! It was fun! Time for you!

Oh come on!
Oh come on!

Please take it!
It's all for you!

I don't know what to do! I don't know what to say! I don't know how to live, my soul's not changing!

It's not changing! No!

It's not changing!

It's for me, not for you! I want it back, what did I do! Yeah!

My soul is gone, I wonder why I sold it to the man for dimes?

Live my life day by day!

Sin by sin in a haze!

I'm dropping bombs, baby, I'm fucking going crazy!

I'm dropping bombs, baby!

Please someone, please save me!

I don't know! No, I don't know! I don't know what to do, don't know what to say! I don't know how to live, my soul's not changing!

It's not changing!

It's not changing!

All Mine

I just had to stop you walking by and I had to tell you you're pretty fine!

> Now I have you!
> Now I have you!
> All mine!

Here I go now!

I knew by the way that you looked in my eyes that this was the beginning to a new life. I wasn't even looking, you caught me by surprise!

> Now I have you!
> Now I have you!
> All mine!

Now I'm the kind of guy who doesn't like wasting time; I'm counting the hours as they go by, 77.5 hrs, no lie. I'm pretty sure that it was love at first sight! Life is pretty tough at times but you make it alright!

> Now I have you!
> Now I have you!
> All mine!

I wish I could turn back the hands of time and have met earlier in life. But all I can do is cherish our time! And keep on planning out our new lives.

> Now I have you!
> Now I have you!
> All mine!

Now the way we feel, trust me, it's alright, no one can change our set minds! I'm strapped in for every ride. Whether it's fast or slow, we will survive! Don't ever leave me and don't ever go. No one knows what's down that road. The road of

love and our souls! Oh baby, I love you so!
Now I have you!
Now I have you!
All mine!

Now the beginning to life is the easiest thing! Days go by and I try to change! No one knows where it might be. The answer to my life and that one key!
    Now the beginning of life is the easiest thing!
        Days go by and I try to change!

No one knows what it's all about. I'm searching my life and I need some help! Help from above! Or another contract from hell!
I'm lost in this life, please someone help!
Now the beginning of life is the easiest thing!
Days go by and I try to change!
Now I'm a quarter of the way in and I wouldn't change a thing. I learn from my mistakes and I feel my pain! Life can be so hard and it can be so mean! The meaning to life must be a glorious thing!
Now the beginning of life is the easiest thing!
Days go by and I try to change!
Now the road less traveled is the one I take! I'm running out of money, I'm on an empty tank!
Now if life was so good I would have some change! Some change to me! Some change to my name! Out on the road is where the stories are told! Everyone's looking for their rainbow and gold!

I've been a whining, I've been a crying! But I've been drinking booze!

These days are getting longer and life's getting shorter and I got nothing to lose!

I'm playing harder and I'm playing fast, I'm hitting this bottle like it's my last!

I've been a whining, I've been a crying! But I've been drinking booze!

Here we go!

Times are tough and times are real. When I'm drinking I'm looking for the deals. Playing this life like it's the last! I'm at the bar looking for a blast!

I've been a whining, I've been a crying! But I've been drinking booze! Times are changing and times are real! The past is gone but the past I can't steal! Days have come and days have passed. I'm digging in my pocket. Where is my flask!

I've been a whining I've been a crying! But I've been drinking booze!

7 x 12

I am stuck, trapped, locked down! Get me out! I've got myself in this hard spot, a 7x12 concrete slab of pain! No tears for the wicked, but the wicked is why I'm here!

I must reflect, rewind my life! No, just start a new chapter, you fool! Don't look back! These walls are just the beginning. They shall not come down on me! I shall come out of them! Wow, something I want to leave so badly and can't handle the confinement! Is this what is changing me and making me a better man? Show no fear! Take what you have within that 7x12 cell and cherish it, love it, and know it!

You!

Addiction

I've had a taste for a long time! This taste has come and never left. It's all around me and I fell for it when I couldn't see to find another way!

So many flavors to ease my troubled mind, and to hide from my true reflection! A waste of my life!

Addiction, you have taken me away from myself and others! No! Never again! This is my life and it now tastes a lot better than you ever have! I know who I am now and now I finally see the real you!

Doesn't have to be a daily fix or a rock-bottom moment! The weekend thrills are enough to destroy a man! You almost had me, that bitter but yet so sweet taste and feeling you gave me! This new flavor is the only spice of life and I thank God I found it!

Sobriety!

Learn!

Learn from your mistakes, learn! This can't be that hard, come on now! Didn't like how it felt, did you? The sting, the sore, the infection! Heal! To learn and not repeat is the only way to move forward! So move on, take the knowledge, and put it in front of you so when you come to the fork, the point, or the ledge you will have the sign in front of you, pointing you in the right direction.

No U-turns! Take your time; life is short. Come to a crawl if you must. Take it in, enjoy, remember, and never forget what keeps you moving forward! The reminder of the sting, the sore, the infection. These all show pain and knowledge. The healing key!

Learn!

Time

Time is ticking, time is tocking, and time is always wasting! One time a year we gain an hour. But only just to give it back. Later in the year! Life is broken down into years, months, days, hours, minutes, and seconds. Time is forever way too short but at the same time infinite! Some days fly by, some days drag, but all twenty-four hours to the second! Why?

We punch in at work, we punch out to record our time put in! We set our clocks, watches etc. . . . to be on time. We try to pass time, waste time, or make time!

Time is life; don't waste time for then you are wasting your life.

Crossover

I feel the tingle, the warmth, the change!
Something is going on inside my soul; can it really be what I've not known or understood for so long?

The evil has had a hold on me for as long as I can remember! I've run with the beast, the sick of the sick, and the sadness for what? A life of pain?

I was given a chance to hide from him and look deep into my mind, my body, and my soul. Searching a higher me and power!

This is the crossover to the pure, the honest, and good life! I shall not give it a name for I just can't explain the shock and joy I'm feeling, but God knows his work! I'm not afraid anymore of anything, I've stopped and just given myself the time, the thought to see the other side and it's just the beginning but I'm sure it's going to be a lot better than running toward the end!

GOD BLESS!

The Mind of the Real!

To be true to myself, that is the only part of my life that I've battled! Honesty to others, yes! But lies to myself no more! To be real you must stand up for what you believe in. Be true to yourself and love! This is the mind of the real!

Everything happens for a reason! You may not like it but there is a plan for us! If I was there . . . This would have happened, or if I just would have stayed home. If we could just channel the plan life would be perfect! Wow, the easy street. Yeah right, not for this guy! I chose the hard way! And that's OK! What I've done has made me sharp!

Now from here on out, what I do will make me sharper! Leave no room for mistakes and I won't have any! Yes, I know nobody's perfect, but at least that rule of thumb will keep them to a minimum.

Greed

We want what we want! We need what we need! We give what we don't, and we waste what we can't! Some want a lot and some don't! The greed is our ruin! So to just use, to survive, and to smile is a generous way of life. Giving is a great feeling, as is to receive. One hand does wash the other in this world of greed and selfishness! Try it! To just take, take, take! Is why we are in gridlock, and the rich are richer and the poor are stealing. As if there isn't enough to go around. Please, dirt is free and so is the rain and sun! Therefore why the hell do we pay for food! Greed is the ruin, and to give will overpower greed if we try!

Tomorrow

I'm unsure of tomorrow! I'm afraid, scared, the unknown, it's a foot upon my chest! I can't breathe! I'm so tense at times, can't live within my own skin! That's got to be the demons within that I'm pushing out finally! It's a war, me against hell. Tomorrow's going to come! I know because I have faith. I will win this war and what tomorrow brings will allow me to breathe!

One thought, one goal, one step at a time! I will succeed!

They will try to hold onto me. They will try to take me down with them. Wow, it's so hard, because the sin is all I've known for as long as I saw the sun rise in my life. There's a plan and it's with me; I must stay focused to see it clearly! I've got the answers to this war! Who's going to win? Tomorrow will tell, and the future will hold my tomorrow's forever more if I succeed to do what faith and tomorrow brings.

One thought, one goal, one step at a time!

Drugs, No!

Drugs, they do what they do! And they do us! Do us in! Do us out!

Do us in trouble, and do us without! A lot of travels to our destination. To our goals of peace and harmony.

Drugs bring me up, drugs bring me down. I wouldn't be in this situation if drugs were not around! They will not go away but I must know!

Know when to leave and when to say no!

To Be Cleansed

My soul is cleansed from the dirt, the rotten, the foul! Run out like a dirty rag. Drip drop! It is dry! Like a new sponge ready to soak up the new! But this time I'm wiping up a pure, clean, and simple puddle!

Souls are written and not duplicated! But yes, they can be cleansed!

There comes a point when you can't take the smell anymore and there is time for a change! Change for me and everybody around me will reap the benefits of the cleansing and purity of my inner, my outer, my heart, my soul!

So Far Down!

Minutes away from falling! So far down, the thought of getting back up seems so impossible! Everything I've worked for and my shelter is about to slip down below my feet.
So far down, so far down!

I guess this is my bottom! Rock bottom, yes! I'm below the rock! It's on top of me; I need strength to get it off of me, and to start climbing up out of this dark, damp, unknown hole!
So far down so far down!

Must rise to my feet, get up! Get up! This is not the end but a lesson to the beginning! So many times I've hit a bottom and wondered if that was the pit? The wretched? Deep down I kind of knew it could always get worse and I let it! Why? It's not like I need a hobby of starting over! I just needed to finally hit the point of almost no return! Return to what? I hope never to fall again and to set that rock up on a ledge and work on climbing even higher than my own life. The top! And sit on that once-rock bottom! A peak of life, an overlook of life, and a million miles of distance to that once dark, damp, unknown hole weighted down by that rock!
So far down, so far down!

How About You?

Something to live for! Something to cherish! Something to love!

Something to inherit! Life is a beauty! Yes, indeed! Life can be ugly if you don't believe! We all inherit life, the day of our coming!

That is an easy day, one so pure! The days that follow are the ones we need to cherish! Find something to live for! Something to inherit! I got it!

How about you?

Myself!

I knew someday I would find the brighter side of my life! These pages in my past were sinful and real!

Yes, I learned the hard way, but it got me to the point to write a brighter, much happier side of this story of life and knowledge and the struggle I came across!

Pages to chapters to books they will come! Life is a story. Sad or unbelievably great! Its days and months of constant days and months of sadness and happiness and days to come! I knew someday I will find myself! Keep myself, know myself.

For the constant days and months to come will be great and fulfilled to the time I have none!

Outside These Walls

The air is so fresh today, the sky so blue! The sun shining down on me! This day I'm so true! I soak up the sun, for the time I can do! I breathe in the air, this is my fuel!

The sun pierced my eyes for days I've not seen! The air made me light headed for it is so clean!

Everyday senses that people take for granted I only had an hour this week and it felt everlasting! Outside these walls is a world I've known. Taking away confined from home! To get a glimpse of earth's giving just made me realize how much I'm missing! Things I've seen for twenty-seven years were enough for a grown man to almost drop some tears.

Outside these walls is where I'll soon be! Being taken away one day or thirty! It's outside these walls that I must journey! Outside these walls is a life worth seeing, a life worth living, and a life worth having. Once I get outside these walls, this life I shall never take for granted!

How Are You Today?

Hello! How are you today? I'm fine! I woke up, so far so good! What are you going to do today? I'm going to do right no matter what I do! That's great, you got it in you don't you? I sure do! If I didn't nobody else is going to do me right! I must always take care of myself and everything else will follow! My loved ones, my assets, my dreams! Hello! How are you today?

I'm on top of the world! Just by doing right the world is now mine! From here on out! Hello, how are you doing today? I shall always answer, I'm fine!

Dreamer

They can be so clear, my thoughts, and visions! I'm a dreamer!

It's an escape from reality brought on by sleep! Also to sleep a lot, to escape, is a sign of depression! But I'm not depressed, I'm just chasing my dreams the cheapest way I know how! I'm a dreamer! I can be anyone I want to be! I can analyze the future through them! Why don't I turn my dreams into reality? This life! Not my conscious channel, my dreams. Think deeply that they will and are to happen! Some are so vivid, some I don't remember, some I repeat! What is this world beyond my inner self? Dreams are thoughts, goals as well as visions; some we understand, some we are clueless! I am a dreamer! Never forget my dreams, goals, thoughts, visions, etc. . . . For soon I will be living in my dreams and I shall be awake and in my life only to be chasing my new dreams to come! I am a dreamer! I won't ever stop! There are times when my dreams are all I got!

I am a dreamer!

What If?

What if? What if? What if?
Wow! That's a good question! What if what?
All the things I wish I would have done or have had, only what if? This is a question that is so right to ask but so destructive to deal with the answers to it. The brain damage, what if? Causes! But we do it all the time! I personally try not to even ask what if? I roll with the punches as they come; 100,000 fists of pain I'd rather take the guilt-driven, stomach-dropping feeling that one question can cause a person. What if? What if I would have just took such a powerful question and applied it before the action or situation and took the better or longer end of the straw and everything would be peachy! The brain damage, that guilt-driven, stomach-dropping feeling what if causes! Will never ever be asked or used down the road of this life I asked what if?

Winning Hands

Some hands are great! Some hands are OK! Some hands you just can't win! This was the hand I was dealt. These cards just won't take a hand. A hand to help me up, a hand to pat my back, and a hand to shake! I need a hand to win! Misdeal! Play the cards you were dealt! Don't be afraid! Life's a game; we all must play it! Some just get by! Not this time! I got the cards to win it! Play to win this game of life. Even with the worst hand! I know I can manage to get a few! Some hands to help me up, some hands to pat my back, and a hand to shake! Those were the cards I was dealt. But now I got a strategy to win this game. My hands will then be free of those cards, and I'll have my own hands to help me up, to pat my back, and a hand to shake! Those were the cards I was dealt! And now I got the winning hands!

Go Get It!

I've lost everything! My actions and sins have caught up to me! I've lost everything! I have a few goals and very little cash and a woman thousands of miles away! This is going to be the biggest challenge of my life and if I do it right it shall be my last! I've lost everything! So let's see here, my goals I must apply ASAP! My little cash I must save! My woman thousands of miles away I must get to as soon as I get everything in order to be comfortable there! I've lost everything!

Come on now, you got your health! You got those goals, and be lucky you still got that woman! You're not dead! You got more than most! Apply that mind of yours! Think you're a survivor, you know you can do this! What doesn't kill you only makes you stronger! So they say! OK you should be stronger than an ox then! Go on, go get it! Get everything you want and need! Sometimes we must lose everything before we get everything! So go on! Go get it!

One Second!

Why me? I didn't sign up for this! I didn't ask for it, and I didn't buy a raffle ticket to win it! God, if I could only take it back! It only took one stupid decision to change my life in a second! At this moment it's not for the better either! But maybe down the road I will say differently! Lost it all! One decision, one second, one lost life! Start all over! Find it! It might only take a second to get it back and the way the thinking was going I doubt a stupid decision is going to work! Think smart! Seconds come and go, grab one and make that second one that lasts a lifetime!

Machine My Mind

Sixteen days into this new mind of mine! I was so lost with drugs for so long I forgot who I was. So wild and crazy! Now as the days go by I'm starting to realize my mind is so beautiful without the escapes I've loved for so long. Who am I? There are moments of such extreme energy and creativity that flood my mind with these words! I believe I've opened my mind to the point of no return. I've created my mind, I've molded it to be a machine of such beauty that no one can explain! Well I never let anybody in to figure out how it works. For it's mine! It's only been sixteen days, so much time left to analyze this machine, my mind!

Pieces and Problems

This is my way, I know! I've been searching! I've been searching the highs! I've searched the lows! I got this life in the bag but there are too many holes. Filled to the top, I can't take anymore! My way has overflowed, and I hit the floor. Pieces and problems that lay! Chaos and confusion you may! Never know what's to come only to see what has passed! Pieces and problems that lay!

Piece by piece I put together only to do it again! I hang onto the last piece for fear, when I put it together it collapses! Jenga! I think everyday now a lot clearer than the chaos and confusion! I'm searching for a bond to hold myself together! For I shall never collapse! This is my way, I know! Problems come and problems go! I've found that bond, now I shall hold! Hold together for problems to come. That bag of holes now has none! Strong enough to hold me for the days to come! Pieces and problems! None!

Give to Get

    I'm going to have it all! Everything I want! My woman, my health, my career! I'm going to have it all. I'm feeling it! It's the best feeling ever! I'm going to have it all! You know when you just know! That's what I got going on inside these days. God's talking to me; he always has been. I'm finally listening! You got to give to get! But you must give good to receive good! I can't wait! I'm going to have it all! Why can't everybody just feel this way and achieve it all! It's most likely a gift! You got to give to get!

My Love

I think of her every second of every minute of every hour of every day! She's so far away from me yet so close to my heart. My love! The pain that comes with the distance—God I must be with her soon! The fear of losing her! Tearing me apart! My love! Never knew a love so real! Soul mates separated! No way am I not going to let it be true! My love! The warmth that her presence brings me! It's something I crave! It's my best addiction! My love! Time is not or is never on a man's side! And when it comes to love I want all the time in the world to be with. My love! She knows who she is and how precious she is to me! Soon enough this test will prove! My love! For I can't live this life without! My love!

She said to me that I can be a better man and I would succeed! That I had it in me, and didn't need the buzzed mind, and the evil inside! I'm glad she saw it in me and I thank God I'm alive!

Twenty-twenty vision I have and couldn't see! It took her eyes to pull me aside and tell me! I looked back into her eyes and started to cry! Thank you for showing me and giving me confidence that I couldn't see! All those drugs and evil had a hold on me.

Take Care

Never say good-bye! Take care is to let good-bye go! Never say good-bye! You never want to think that you will never take another look at someone again! Take care of yourself and your heart will know what to do! Never say good-bye to something that is good to you! Never say good-bye to someone your heart desires! Take care of your heart as I did mine for years. I'm never going to say good-bye because I'm forever yours! Take care is to let good-bye go! Take care of today! Take care of our hearts, for when we're together we'll never part! Take care!

No Maybes

You only get one life, no maybes! You got to keep moving and changing! Life could be so good yet amazing! If you believe! You only get tomorrow and what's coming! You got to grab on now, no running!

This life is so fast, now so crazy! It took some things now to save me!

You only get one life, no maybes! Get everything you want now and save it. Don't take anything now for granted! If you succeed now you'll have it! You got to hold on now! Oh baby! I'm doing the best I can now, don't leave me! I finally got a vision and wow! I can't wait to have it! Soon it will be now! You only get one life, no maybes! Life could be so good yet amazing! If you believe!

New life! New career! New state! New friends! New clothes! New me! New me, I can't wait to start all over and choose my path in life! You don't get too many chances to do this! It's like being born again but knowing right from wrong! New life!

The Good

Tell me, come on! Say it! I want to hear it! What? I want to hear what I want to hear. People love to hear what they want to hear. So find out their kicks, their poisons, feed them! They're all ears! Listen up, people, these words are good! Feel good! Make good! People feed off the good feeling! So to tell good, to make good, they will feel good! And if they are feeling good! They are now in the circle of the good life and it's not going to stop as the wheel turns and passes the good feeling this life brings! Tell me, come on! Say it! I want to hear it! I want to feel it and spread it.

The Good!

One day away from the beginning!
One day away from the new!
One day away to freedom!
I can say I know what to do.

I got a master! I got a teacher if you will! To give me guidance and let me know what to do. One day away to myself and it feels so pure and true! Every day is now going to be one day that I know I'll be true. True to myself and my teacher, who passes me through this life, that I now have one day left to finally do!

Dreams come and go and some you will never know the meaning of life and the paths we follow. But to follow those dreams that come are the ones you will always remember! Hang on to them!

Dreams

What do they mean? They are so vivid! My only escape from me! From this place! The only connection I have to my loved ones and my goals! What do they mean? Is it true what they say? Dreams do come true?

Five Months Ago

She walked in and sat down. Her hair was amazing, so full, so sexy! I wanted to stare but didn't want to be obvious! She had to be mine! I've never seen such beauty! The excitement I had as I moved close to her! It was perfect! Conversation and attraction were flowing as if we both knew at that moment what was to come of us! Love at first sight? Maybe!

It was five months ago today that my life changed and my heart beat again! Five months ago today seems so long ago, as if I've had a lifetime of love and happiness all in five months! Life has slowed down! That's perfect! Love could be the fountain of youth! True love! Five months ago today was the beginning of something that only her and I can explain, and as the months go on I still stop myself to take in the moment she walked in and sat down five months ago!

Never let you go

She walked into my life, never wanted to leave!
She's been taken away; she's been taken from me!
It's the love for me, it's the love for her!
She's the air I breath, she's my everyday; in this world I live she's my everything!

This love for me, this love for you is real!
Going to break me, break me down to size!
Oh baby never realized!

Never! Never! Never let you go!
Never! Never! Never let you go!

This life is going to never let you down!
It's going to start shining now!
From days to months to years they will fly by!
Just as long as I got you by my side.
And the world will see in the eyes of envy it's you and me!

It's the simple things that you do for me!
It's the way I catch you looking at me!
You take me in with every sight.
It's the passion we have in the dawn of the night!

This love for me this love for you is real!
Going to break me, break me down to size!
Oh baby, never realized!

Never! Never! Never let you go!
Never! Never! Never let you go!

Now this world can be a hard place!
And it all goes away when I look at your face!
From that sexy hair to those beautiful browns.
Not to mention when you turn around!

Meeting you has been a beautiful thing.
I still stop and think about that day!
And the eye contact to what's your name!
This true love is a beautiful thing.

This love for me, this love for you is real!
Going to break me, break me down to size!
Oh baby, never realized!

Never! Never! Never let you go!
Never! Never! Never let you go!

She walked into my life, never wanted to leave!
She's been taken away; she's been taken from me!
It's the love for me, it's the love for her!
She's the air I breathe, she's my everyday!
In this world I live she's my every thing!

We don't know!

We don't know about the things and the people we see!
We don't know about this life and what it holds for you and me.
We don't know!
Life is a ticking and rotating time clock. What time is it?
We don't know!

Rock Star

Rock star turning demented minds!
Laying and laughing, blowing my mind!
Pushing the limit, blowing lines!
Rocking, rolling all the time!
Woman and woman in the line!
Piles and piles of cash no more
Searching, searching for the piece on the floor!
Lost in the carpet this world no more!

Status of life

There's times in my life I feel as if I'm going to make it! Be of some meaning to life! Accomplish all my goals, rise to the top! The top of what? The status of life? Or the level of what people of a successful class see me as? Then all those feelings are swept out from under my skull and seem so far away because I'm even farther away from where I was when I felt them. Maybe I'm closer to them and unsure of the process or the feelings I'm to have as I reach the status of life! So far I've never been there! I just hope when I get there I will realize it and hang on to whatever it is even if it's just one split second that I feel it! At least I know next time how it feels!

What am I waiting for? I guess if I knew I wouldn't be asking this question! Just wasting time! It's not like it's on my side! I'm on borrowed time as it is! So what is it? Why am I wasting what everybody else is trying to save?

Take what I got and use it! To the fullest and beyond if I can!

Time will tell what it is used for and then it will be on my side to figure out my next move!

They take me and tell me I did wrong! But in my eyes I'm just alive! In this movement I can't hide! Will someone come along and save me from my sins?

They lurk in me everyday! I can't fight them all alone! These days just flying by! Fighting demons getting high!

There's no direction to this life, hiding behind a mirror of pain and suffering!

Everyday I'm in! Is another day without! Pain and suffering!

In this world I'm just alone! It's for me, it's not for you!

The Kiss

All I can think about is the kiss. The first one! And the one I'm about to have! I want it so bad! Soft, firm, and passionate! To just take her in with pure passion and love! To hold her with my arms! She's pressed against my body, my hand on her face! I caress her lips with the power of mine! Pure ecstasy! Nothing matters at that moment we share! Our lips bind together as if they were one! Everything is spinning and passing us by as we stand there in complete heaven with one another! I want to open my eyes but just for a second to look at such beauty. I do that at times just to slip away again into our trance. It's all I can think about and I know it will be soon. I could give up everything else in this life to have that moment forever! All I can think about is the kiss! The one moment I'm about to have, and a lifetime of them to come!

On My Way

There was hope there was a chance! Today was to be my beginning! My freedom! It never came today! There are a few turns I must take before I get there! Tomorrow will be my first left to right! Right to do from this day on and days to come! There are so many, and so much wrong! Turns and ways to go! To be clear and honest with myself and others is a path that will take me to the place I've wanted for so long! I just had to stop here to gather a few more things to take with me! I'm packed and on my way!

Saved

It's a strange feeling to be put in a cage and have to adapt to a new way of life. It's safe from temptation and sin but hard to be away from loved ones and freedom to enjoy the fruits of life. I don't hate myself for being here. I've been saved! Saved from myself! Saved from others! Saved from the evil that is around everyday life. It's always going to be there. I love how I'm feeling away from it. It's a pure life for my mind, body, and soul! And when I'm free to the world I'm taking this serenity with me. Sometimes it takes hard times to realize what's good for you! In my case it's been a few. There's a reason for all of this. Just know when it's going on! If you wait too long it will be too late! To be saved comes with time! Once you are, life will show itself, as for the meaning and the reason you were saved.

Enough Is Enough

I've been given many chances. I've been saved from the worst of times! I could never realize when enough is enough. Now I'm in a position that I've never wanted to be in. This could have been avoided! It can be worse! This is another wake up call! It has to be the last. There's a lot in my life I want to do! I was put here to analyze my life, test myself! Fight myself again. I'm doing just that. It's hard to see the future when put away from the present! I have faith in myself and my higher power! That's what is keeping me sane, and every day in is one closer to out. I must be patient! If I rush this time I won't get all that is to come out of it! With time all good things shall come. Enough is enough! Chances don't always come! As hard as this one is it still is a chance. So when is it safe to say enough is enough?

The first chance you get!

True Love

Everyone has their own feelings on love, about love and the experience of love. There are different levels people experience and believe that what is felt is love. Is it really? If one hasn't experienced different levels then they may not know what love is. You can say you have felt it! Then down the road you meet that person that blows your mind away and your heart! You have never felt this before! So you tell yourself this must be it! True love at last! I know I got it! This is what I've wanted for so long. It's a combination of things that can't be beat by anything! It's solid! No evil or temptation on this earth will break it! It's so amazing! True love is a key to life! For mine! Once you find it hang on to it! I know I'm going to. I don't want to look back and wish I had it. True love!

Thirty-Eight Days

Thirty-eight days in this place away from the world. My heart is broken today, my strength is down. I'm fighting back the tears. My question to when I will be home isn't being answered, nor do I have the hope! Some days are harder than others. Today is the hardest! Thinking about my son, my girl, and my life now, and what it's to be. This time wasn't planned and the duration of it is unknown. Day after day! One at a time. It's just me and my mind, questions and answers and thoughts to come! It's a challenge and I'm unsure of the reason but know it's for a good one.

Thirty-eight days gone but not wasted! Every second of each day was well spent in my head to prepare for my next. Tomorrow must be better than today and thirty-eight days gone is better than the next to come! They are behind me! Over! And done!

Enamored

I didn't know how to say it to her! The days and nights we spent together just built up this feeling inside that I didn't know could happen so fast.

From the first walk in the woods! As I took her in, with my eyes, and ears! To the evening in the car drinking beers! The moments that followed the lust in the air!

The dates that followed, the bike path through the woods! The blankets under the stars! The kissing, the touching, just like we knew we would! Oh and the fire we started for such a short time it lasted! It was the hours that followed that kept this love everlasting!

I didn't know how to say it to her! I was afraid to say it. I didn't want to express my feelings too soon. Like a flower waiting to bloom. But with her I didn't care! I went from the three words to just one! Enamored, yeah, that's the one! I'm not sure I spelled it right! That's exactly what I said when I told her that night.

Enamored: to be inspired with love. That's how I told her the first night I fell in love! Now I tell her that I love her! But it took just one word to start this love to last forever!

The Plan

I don't have one, I wish I did! Tomorrow isn't even in my head. I got goals and dreams but not in play! I'm not sure if I can put them on a day! I just let faith control them. At the same time I need to have a hold of them. How can I plan out the unknown? Everything changes with time and seasons! The plan is a structured life to who already has lived.

One idea to the next in my head! I need a plan! The plan! Life isn't meant to be. I believe. That would take out all the fun and excitement to the plan one has for me! It's not in my hands. The plan lays in the hands and mind of your higher power! You need to listen to him, obey him! Don't get lost! Don't disobey! Stay true and righteous to thee! The plan he has you will one day see! So the plan that you think you need! It's simple!

You just got to believe!

Myself

Do I know? Do I lead? Do I carry out my wants and needs! Do I do myself?

There are things I need to do! Dreams, goals, and paths to follow! I can't get caught up in the patterns of others or everyday life! It takes away from myself! My life!

To do myself, my inner thoughts, my outer desires! I must do what I believe is in me to do, and stop saying tomorrow!

Paranoid

What am I paranoid about? Life is against me! No way it's on my side! Paranoia will destroy you! Looking through the windows! Shutting off the phones! They are coming! Who? I don't even know what I'm worried about! These feelings coming over me! There's no reason I'm in harm's way! How did they find me? Who sent them? What for? They are not outside, they are not on the phone! They are not watching me! They are in me! How? Why? Who are they and what do they want? Quiet, I hear something! I'm paranoid! Or are they? Please stop! Stop talking to me! Who are you!

I'm Paranoid!

Me

I can't sit! I can't stand! I'm walking! Talking! Unsure if I want to sit or what to do? I'm lost, I'm confused! What's my next move? Why am I restless? A lot on the mind! Can't point it out! I'm going to find the reason to all this! I must keep on this path of being lost! Wow, this sucks, I need directions! Wait, I'll just write it out! That's the best way to ride it out! Answers and answers to no questions! None of this makes sense! I'm no better than the beginning of this. I can't sit! I can't stand! I'm lost and confused! I can't write, I have nothing! Nothing to calm or ease my troubled mind! Running around and nowhere to hide! The questions I have I made them up in my head! Circles and twists to throw at myself! I guess that's the way to find myself. One question, many answers! It's not just the unknown that eats at a man! Must stay calm and relax! I know I can! So many directions will be clear and not lost! I'll be at ease! Just got to stop and realize and stay focused on me! Everything else is what it is and will always be. At the end of this the answer is me!

Serenity

There are times when things seem impossible! Too much stress, heartache, and confusion! These are issues we have with life! There are many ways to mask how we feel. Run from our issues or fight our battles! Are they safe? Are they relaxed? Are they above a level we have never experienced? I want that! Is it a feeling or a place? Serenity, is it a place to hide? A feeling inside? That we must find in a way that once we do our lives will be at the highest point one may experience?

Serenity isn't going to come to me! Serenity is there! It isn't far away! But you can't see it, and you won't feel it if you put yourself around the same feelings that are chaotic! I'm there, I believe I have found it! It's a feeling of ease and trouble free! No matter how hard this life is it's a way to see! Serenity—to have it means it's within you! For years to come! It's found within and will always be. That feeling you have been searching for! That place to hide! You cannot see!

Serenity!

Wasted

There's no reason to hide! To run away, to become annihilated from my own self being! But I find a way! From that first drink, that white line, that pill! Those ups and downs, those feelings of complete euphoria! It's so easy to want to go there! But what's the reason for this? Hard times go! Good times are what you make them! To get wasted and wretched in one's own mind is a mirror of life; it's still there, it's not going to vanish! Time is going to fly by and nothing will be done with life by taking the highway home! Having a clear mind is the best way to see things clearly! To get things done that you need to in life. Getting wasted is just that! A waste! A waste of time, money, power, and success! Not to mention yourself!

There's a right way and a wrong way to get all that one can out of his or her life! It takes a lot of wrongs sometimes and the times you have wasted you can't get back! So don't waste anymore! Use every second of everyday and look from present to future! The wasted are over and will not last! For tomorrow is brighter and clearer, and the wasted is in the past!

Stand by Me

There are times when life can throw us twists and turns! Stand by me. There are moments of triumph! Stand by me.

Stand by me as you should know I will for you! No matter what is going on, I'm there for you!

Don't ever doubt that my word isn't real and know that we are equal and what's to be done shall come for both of us. As we are one! Stand by me.

We are us, no other can compare! This love and bond that is so true gives us the directions on what we need to do. At times we will be scared but that is life! Stand by me. As I will for you for the rest of my life!

Take Me Away

95 to 85, I hit the road, it's time to drive!
Never looking back!
Never looking back!
Never looking back!
Roads ahead of me, life's behind me!
I hit the road.
Never looking back!
Never looking back!
Never looking back!
Take me away now, baby, take me away!
This life I live but refuse to change!
Trucking down the road, searching for better days!
Take me away!
Take me away!

She's so beautiful! Her hair, the way it flows like gold in a river. So wild and brown! With streaks of gold! She's so beautiful! Her browns pierce me as she looks at me so attentive and strong. I throb for her. She's so beautiful! Her body moves with confidence and strength, protecting her young and claiming her man. She's so beautiful! Her heart is strong and giving. Never to be broken! The passion she has and the love she gives.

  She's so beautiful!

Can't Stop Thinking!

Can't stop thinking! Why? If I stop my days are done! Can't stop thinking! The race is on; every thought that fills my mind is running in and away. Can't stop thinking! Every thought must be analyzed! Thought out and played out! Like a game I want to win!

To be seen as somebody I'm not! My appearance doesn't mean anything when the words are written black and white. Words of disappointment, words of crime! Words! Black and white!

My kindness, my heart, my life! Words! Black and white!

Pain

As I live and have things in my life happen, things of joy, things of pain! I get through the things of pain but forget what it was that caused that pain. The actions that got me to the point of heartache, loss, and gut-wrenching, knife-twisting tears dripping from my soul pain!

I must never forget the things that I've done and the feelings I have from them. That feeling of pain will soon then leave and the feelings of joy I will have and live for everyday!

In the Middle of Life

The beginning was easy. The end is unknown. The middle is the hardest life that I have ever known! The middle of time! The middle of age! This middle-life crisis, if you may. I'm not halfway but a quarter in. I'm in the middle of life until the end!

Words

They come as they do. Some are many, some are few. Some are loud, some are quiet. The ones that are not spoken are silent. Choose them wisely for you don't want to eat them! Let them flow and people greet them. These words of wisdom, these words of days. Must be the reason to life this way! Make it easy! Make it real! Choose the words you use, and seal the deal!

Hard Times

It's not easy! Oh no! It's not! It's the shit that's hard that gets me. Gets me lost, gets me tight and twisted up. The hard times! Oh yes! They are not easy! Doing hard time, stuck between a rock and a hard place. Whatever it may be, hard times will get the best of you. Everything is breakable. Everything! I can break or it can be broken.

Break them! Break them before they break you! Breaking the hard times is the only way to get you through!

To have a life full of love, joy, and freedom! To have a life!

Stuck Here

Stuck here, where am I? In a place of many but all are lost. Stuck here! Wandering souls in search for a breeze, some air someday. Stuck here! To close my eyes is my escape. Walking amongst the strong, but weak to reality! Stuck here! Where am I? Once I find myself in a place where I am, I will no longer be lost. My soul will breathe the air it has, and the breeze I need will carry me away!

I know who I am. Do you? I know what I'm here for. Many places are here. The one you know is the one you have yourself in. So do you really know who you are? Do you really know yourself? Do you really know where you are? The one place is here. Inside yourself!

Positive Goals!

The positive thoughts I have are what get me by. They make me feel good! They become goals. Positive goals! Now how do I achieve them? I can think them and that feels amazing! Imagine if I achieve them. Positive goals!

They became a part of my day as I became at one with myself. I had to sit down away from society to grab them. I have a tight grip on them now! Positive goals! Now I must release one finger at a time until those positive goals fit in the palm of my hand!

Drive Thru World

We pull around the buildings. This world! We wait in line, this world. Not fast enough! One lane at a time! It's quick in our minds. Our lazy minds! Our lazy world! One window at a time to get what we need. Some faster than others, some better than others, some cheaper than others. This world! This drive thru world! Serve me, window! Serve me good! This drive thru world! I knew you would!

Breathe

I'm ready to go. The thoughts of what may happen, good or bad, are upon me. I can't breathe! Breathe, take a deep breath, remain calm. Everything is going to be OK. OK for me, OK for my well-being. No matter what happens, breathe! I still have a lot of that left! I am ready to go, good or bad, I am ready! With every breath I take for everyone, mine! Breathe in and everything will be fine! Breathe!

Sunshine

The sunshine beats down upon me! Every ray I soak in! This UV word, my UV soul, my soaked up battery of life! Let it shine upon me, let it fuel my soul, let it heat my heart, for this sunshine I now have in my life and shall never part!

Freedom

To escape is the only way. The only way out of this illegal society! My way, or the hard times! I'd rather have it my way than day-to-day sadness and heartache. Both are not easy. Love and family I ache for.

But freedom is my salvation!

Decisions

My decisions I make are for my safety, my pride, my soul. My decisions, they are only mine. So I make them! I make them proud! Proud Decisions!

I'm only one man in this lost place, this third world, if you may, my world! So many things change. My mind, the weather, my days! My time here is easy, a place on Easy Street. Right on the corner of Freedom!

Small Devices

Small things can get to be so powerful! Destruction of your life, the small things! From the handheld device to the soul you cannot see.

The small device has a hold on thee. So who you are can be so small but the inner you is the largest of all! The soul you once had or the one you will never know! Is for the world to see! The smallest of them all!

Eighteen Days

The days went by so fast, eighteen days! One big dream! The ones that you don't remember and the ones you'll never forget! These days one through eighteen!

Every one well spent!

Cash It In

It's almost time to cash in the first part, the only quarter in! So don't stop, go for it all! Cash this hard work, cash this mind, this hard-working mind! Cash it in! It's only a quarter in and the rest will come!

My Civil War

Being in a strange place is a hard time in my life! It is a challenge. To not accept or be accepted when your mind is fighting its heart everyday.

It's a civil war that I must win, and I'm only one man in this war! My civil war! Maybe it's me against the world? My tears are pouring like the ink to this page! This civil war has become a world war I must win! Tears of my fight! Tears! Tears for love! Fight! Win! Tears!

My Civil War!

Hold On

Hold on to everything you have. Even if you leave it, hold on! So tight you will always have, you're everything that you know. Without your everything, you will spend a lifetime searching for nothing you once had.
Hold On!

Losing track of time, losing track of life! What day is it? What's the date? This is insane! So lost, so confused, but so happy!

Destiny

Had a chance to go back! Was in such a blur that I let it slip me by. I'm not ready! I left to be free from my pain of life. But created a different type of pain! I'm going to move forward in my life to find what it is I need! Almost 31 years I've been searching. Searching for me! My destiny! Destiny is all I have! What is my destiny? I know it's not pain! So where is it? And is it now?

Destiny!

Thirty-One Years To Be

May these years pass me by! A day away from another year! Another life! Thirty to thirty-one years in! I'm alive, I'm free, I'm thirty-one years to be!

As the wind blows and the water beats down upon you. May you stay dry and warm as you travel through this world! This jungle unknown!

Everyday that I live and hide is a day I can't live inside of this life that I live in pain; I want this life to feel the same! Never going to leave it again because it's a life of sin!

Ask your soul if you know who you are! Ask if you have met before! Listen to the words and make sense of the answers you hear! You may not like what you hear but at least you got an answer!

When I think of a kiss I think of you! When I think of a hug I think of you! When I think of love I think of you!

The thought of you is love and will never change! The little things that we share are the best feelings I've ever felt! From the soft touches behind the ear, and the nibbles upon the neck and shoulder! This feeling of love for you is becoming stronger as it gets older!

I have a fear I must admit to you! The fear is losing you! Living my life with a hole in my heart! A hole I know I will never be able to fix! A hole I never want to start!

To go on in this life that I must do! To go on without you, I couldn't imagine the pain and suffering I would feel! Trust me when I say! This love is real!

There are times when days fade away; these are few and are in my way! Everyday I can't hide from the pain, the truth of lies! The bars that keep me inside!

There are times when days fade away! Always tomorrow! Never going to keep me away! One man's weakness has become my ruin! My debts will be paid and his lies will come unfolded! My past will be clean, and my memory of these days will fade away!

These days are few and are in my way!

Heartache

Thump! Thump! Slow then fast! It's not normal! It's not steady! Why does it hurt? Why do the tears fall from my eyes! Thump! Thump!

This pain I feel is new; there's been signs of it but never like this! For every beat I choke up! My mind spins! No way out! No way to win! Thump! Thump!

Every beat points to her! Jumps for her! Continues on for her! Hang in there! Thump! Thump! Never stop! Heartache! Never give up! Heartache! This pain I feel is for you, and I will get through ... Heartache!

Boone County

As I wait for my ibuprofen three times a day! Another bologna sandwich, I've lost my way! I pace the floor, I pace my mind! C.O., can I use the phone? Trying to get outside! One day in the unknown to get out!

I sit in Boone County! I scream and shout! I close my own door and I don't know why! I've taken away what freedom I have! Locked up inside!

I order my food, I burn through my cards. I wait for my visits. This makes it less hard! Like a child to a crib I still must ask. To even use the shower! But not to whip my ass!

Are They Coming?

Fourteen days still waiting! Waiting on a ride to close my past! A ride to paradise under lock and key! Two more weeks to see! Are they coming? Are they coming for me? A free ride to the beach, but not for me! To close a case, to close my past! How much time do they have? Two more weeks they got from me! In two more weeks I may see! A sky or a beach is good for me! No matter what, the past is free! Are they coming? Are they coming for me?

These Days

These days go by! I jump into them like a line. One not crossed, but snorted! All these days seem so distorted! One after another they go by! Each a little different, but the same amount of time!

Counting them like bills that go in my pocket! Not like the ones in the mail that are forgotten! So to say that some days are better than others, this is so true! I will count these days till I have no more to do!

At Ease

A major loss for a lifetime of knowledge to my salvation and peace! No matter what is to come from here on out I will be! Everything will be ... At ease!

In this scroll lie the answers to love and the key to happiness! Every word written with a single breath, a single heartbeat! Not every key opens a door, but mine does with you. It fits so perfect, so real, so true! The door to love has opened for us to enjoy, to indulge, but never to destroy!

With this key I keep hidden from the world only to give to you! My love! My girl! There's only one spot I know to hide it! Deep within my heart, where only you can find it! There are many keys to many doors. This one is not just mine but also yours! So now that you know where the key lies. You have the answer to love and happiness for the rest of your life!

So much on my mind! So much time! Not knowing makes it longer than it really is! Must remain calm, must not fight with my mind! Accept the fact that I'm doing time!

Faith

To have fear and challenges and obstacles in your life is OK! It's how you handle them! It's your strength, it's your patience! It's your faith!

Faith is in me! Faith is a part of my daily life! Faith will nourish me! Faith will get me by! Faith is the main ingredient to every recipe of life!

Don't ever doubt it! Don't ever question it! Look, listen, and feel it! For it is all around you! He is showing you and caring for you daily! Take this main ingredient he has given you in life and share it! For it is Faith and the answer to every bit of fear, challenge, and obstacle in life!

Faith!

Does anything really matter at the end of the day? The end of the checkout line? The end of the road? The end of a hard day's work, or a hard day of life? What matters is how you feel before you close your eyes! Did all the money you make or entertainment you enjoyed ease your mind, body, and soul?

How about the excitement of knowing you're on the right road to a better tomorrow from what you received today, not what you wanted! You don't have to work for it! You don't have to want it! You have to just open your eyes and see it! It's all around you! So get in his line! There is no end of this road! This journey goes far beyond your eyes closing for that night or for them to ever open!

So which line are you in and what road have you chosen?

There are many things we need, many things we want! Many things should not be taken for granted upon their arrival! They have come for a reason and it's his reason we have them! Share with one another what we receive, for there's plenty to go around! To be full of something is to fill someone else! He fills me, for he will fill us!

So Small Yet So Big

This cell is measured in feet and inches and is solid and built to confine me! The walls may close in on me only if I allow them to. There is an escape far beyond any release date or bond to be set. He has lifted my mind, my soul! I've found freedom within his words. This cell, so small yet so big! Bigger than the world I've seen. Far beyond these walls I've found my way! My one! My only escape!

In life there are many losses! Many things that we can't explain! Many things that become missing in our lives from which we will be confused or devastated from the moment of our loss! One man's loss is another man's gain! But what did that man gain? Guilt or regret! So material losses can serve as a lesson in life? To lose a loved one is not the same and should be looked at as a gift to God! Something even bigger than the confusion is the outcome and the lesson learned to the loss at hand! Or should I say out of hand?

How much can one man handle? At what point will a man break! Snap, lose control! Fall to the ground and cry! This is the moment of no return! No return to the ways that got you to your knees in tears! This is the breaking point, the turning point of your life! Just enough to seek out and give thanks for the real wake up call, the real turning point! Never more than one man can handle but enough to remember for a lifetime of happiness and a fear of that pain!

I'm being sent on another journey! A journey unknown! Being shuffled like a deck of cards. Pushed into another cell like a herd of cattle! I must not be worried of my destination! Destination unknown! I must have a job to do! One I must keep my eyes open to get. Do the work I'm assigned to! For this journey is for a reason and that reason will show!

I wonder if she is thinking of me! I wonder how she feels! I know how I feel for her! Is she in the same love as I am? Or am I all alone?

Tick Tock

Tick Tock . . . Tick Tock . . . What time is it? What day is it? I don't know! You tell me! I'm in here with you! We're in this time together! Why don't you ask someone else? OK, I will! No one knows! I got the same answer from everyone! Tick Tock . . . Tick Tock . . .

Who are these people? Do you know their names? Do you know why they are here? I don't even know why I'm here but in time I will find out! Tick Tock . . . Tick Tock . . .

My Queen

As these days go by I think of you! All the love we share and the things we do!

Not a day goes by I am alone! You are my Queen next to my throne.

From the romantic nights we share in the room. That's only a taste of how my heart beats for you!

Now to move forward with my Queen by my side! I had to defeat the demons I had inside!

So this time of war that I have won! Has now and will bring our love as one!

So with this, my Queen, hold close to your heart! For this war is almost over! Till death do us part!

On My Way

This life hasn't stopped! This life has had its fair share of days! Everyone on my way!

I've run through many and did not see! Many I've forgotten. Yet many I will be.

On my way to a new life! A new life that sees me! For everything I have learned! On my way!

I'm grateful for my life for everyday is not just for me. I keep these days close to my heart and take them! On my way!

So on my way I will go! Everything I have learned is everything to show!

So I can finally say. I'm on my way. Tomorrow I will learn another day. And take that with me as I go! On My Way! Now I know!

Haters

They gather all around to see with the blind eye! They don't have a clue or a thought that's real inside. Nothing is truer than the envy they have for you.
Haters!

From the time they meet in their own jealous lives. They will try to fend for themselves to feed the greed they hide.
Haters!

For my creator I have by my side! May all you haters step aside! As my doings are pure, real, and true! You can't do for yourselves! You poor pity fools!
Haters!

Guidance

I need you, Lord! I need your guidance today. My head and my heart are at war with the demons I see! Take me, Lord, under your angel's wings with a prayer so strong they fear your name! Your guidance is what I shall follow to see! Follow I will as your guidance leads me! I show no fear as for faith I have! I thank you Lord for your guidance, your path!

I'm at peace with today! Even more for tomorrow! Not a worry in the world! I've found the cure to anxiety, to my troubled mind! It burns so bright within my soul. Now that I found him I will never let go! Thank you, God, for your light that shines! It has always been there, deep inside! Thank you, God, for the cure for me! That light you gave! Now I can see!

I'm at peace with today! Even more tomorrow!

Thank you, God, for your world!

The Devil's Game

Some have danced with the Devil. Some have run with him. The games he's playing, I've played them all! Some have won and many have lost! The Devil's game is the dice being tossed. One to twelve you never gain. He's taking it all, even your name. From the days you play to the numbers that ID you. Sign on the dotted line, he's sure to deceive you! Now the Devil's game, go ahead and play. The losers are winners in the eyes of his game! You will lose; he will try to win. Just remember when I say there's always a way out of this game. This game of sin!

The Florida Keys

The Keys are scattered like the ones floating in the sea! Overboard they went so they won't catch thee. A lot like a web they are to me! One highway in and never free! The Keys are a place to let loose and enjoy but you must look out for the cops! The little blue boys! They know your game and the things you do. As their kids run around to do as they please! The Keys are a place for the police! Now don't get me wrong, the beauty is there! If you can see past the wire fence that keeps you there!

Both Ways!

This love I have is moving forward! So fast, so real, so true! It's not just my way, it's her way too!

The way of love is shared not kept to oneself! A love that goes both ways is a love of wealth!

Now my love is heading your way, I give it all the time! As long as it goes both ways, we're on the same ride.

Love goes both ways, as the saying goes. We feel this love! Both ways! Both ways we know!

This House Is a Circus

I've been to zoos, I've been to parks. I've been to museums where your imagination roams.

I've rode on roller coasters high above city lights. I've snacked on LSD till the end of night.

Nothing compares to this house I stay in! People running and lost in their own heads. The kiddies play as they always do. You can't hear yourself think, as if you want to!

This house is a circus, come on down! There are many ways in! Keep fooling around! They come in all sizes, the costumes they wear! They sleep and make funny noises—crowd beware! The lights stay on till the fat lady sings!

This house is a circus! I've lost my brain!

Vision

To be seen or to never see! What lies for tomorrow, what tomorrow may be! It's right in front of me. My vision not mistaken! With this vision, tomorrow will be taken.

Taken for what is shown or for what you may see! This vision I live is reality! So to see what is to come is a vision so clear!

So tomorrow you won't be afraid, but your vision!
Be Aware!

My Angel

In this life some don't realize what they have. I do!

I've asked many times for God to send me an Angel. To protect me, to bring me love, joy, and a heart so big that my life will change!

My Angel.

I feel the love so deep within my soul. The happiness you bring into my life! The will to do right!

You're my strength when I am weak! My breath when I can't breathe! Your wings wrap around me and keep me safe from the darkness that haunts me! Your embrace!

That hug that fills my heart to its full capacity of love!

You're my Angel! My Angel from above!

My life, my mind have been prisoners of the bottles and baggies of this addictive world!

Is there a love that grows and stands strong! Through the tests of time! The tests of life?

Till the end of time, our time! Time is on our side! This is our time. Our time to love!

Presence

We never take time to be in time! In the moment! Presence! Presence presents!

Presence is a single breath, a single heartbeat! The moment is now! The gift of life! Being is a present from presence!

Time Machine

Traveling back in my mind to days of weeping, nights of laughter. Always looking ahead to a brighter day! A better tomorrow!

A time machine in my mind! Traveling as I'm standing still! A functional time machine! Lost on a journey of thoughts and travels that don't take me anywhere!

The moment I realize the moment! Is a time machine on its own!

Tomorrow

You never know if it's guaranteed. We count on it as a need. Tomorrow comes with us to do. We should be grateful for today and the moments we're in! Just when it comes you do it all again . . . Tomorrow.

Time

Either you're doing time or time is doing you! The only ways to figure out what time it is, is to ask yourself "where am I?" "What am I doing?"

Time!

Ego

Man, you're on top of the world! You're the man! Everybody knows me! I can't get enough of whatever it is I got or I taste. Come on, just another taste won't hurt! Keep doing what you're doing! I'm my biggest fan!

I have an appetite for destruction, some call it a monkey on my back! Some call me the Devil! I'm Ego . . .
Nice to control you!

Days go by, one by one! Months, years, unknown to come!

The time is now, our time to love! The world is in the palm of our hand. The past has returned to love again!

The time between, as if we never stopped! This love still growing, the world on top!

Now hand in hand we will conquer this world! By each other's side, no way can we lose! The past is now present! This love is our proof!

Life is a maze. One to find the way! The way of life one will know. Live for today! Tomorrow unknown!

May your travels bring joy, fortune, and many loves! Just make sure you find life and never get lost!

CPSIA information can be obtained
at www.ICGtesting.com
Printed in the USA
BVHW041630041020
590256BV00014BA/488

9 781478 782162